AI for Rental & Cash Flow Investing

How to Use AI to Build a Passive Income Rental Property Portfolio

By Joe Correa

Published by Live Stronger Faster

This book is for educational and informational purposes only. The author and publisher are not engaged in rendering legal, financial, or other professional advice. Readers should consult a qualified professional before making any financial decisions.

First Edition

Table of Contents

Introduction

The transition from active real estate investing strategies into long-term wealth creation begins with a fundamental shift in mindset. Up to this point in the series, you have learned how artificial intelligence can help you find deals faster, analyze properties with precision, market effectively, and even optimize fix-and-flip opportunities for profit. Now, in Book 6, the focus moves into one of the most powerful and sustainable wealth-building strategies in real estate: rental property investing. This is where real estate stops being a short-term transaction business and becomes a long-term income engine. It is where cash flow becomes predictable, equity begins to compound, and financial freedom starts to take shape through systems rather than constant effort.

Rental investing has always been one of the most reliable paths to wealth, but it has also traditionally been slow, complex, and heavily dependent on experience. Investors had to manually analyze rent prices, study neighborhoods, screen tenants, calculate returns, and manage unpredictable expenses without much data support. Mistakes were costly, and scaling a portfolio often required years of trial and error. Today, artificial intelligence completely changes that equation. AI allows investors to evaluate rental properties in minutes instead of weeks, identify high-cash-flow opportunities before others even see them, and make data-driven decisions that significantly reduce risk. This shift is not just about efficiency—it is about clarity and control in a market that has historically rewarded guesswork.

In this book, you will learn how AI transforms rental investing into a structured, repeatable system. You will discover how long-term rental strategies and DSCR-focused investing can be optimized using intelligent tools that analyze income potential, property performance, and tenant demand. Instead of relying on emotional assumptions or outdated comps, you will begin to rely on real-time data models that show you exactly how a property is likely to perform over time. This includes understanding rental yield, cash-on-cash return, vacancy risk, and long-term appreciation potential—all through AI-assisted analysis that removes uncertainty from the equation.

One of the most important areas of focus in this book is cash flow optimization. Cash flow is the foundation of rental investing, and AI gives you the ability to maximize it in ways that were previously difficult to achieve. From identifying undervalued rental markets to adjusting pricing strategies based on demand trends, AI helps you make smarter decisions that directly increase monthly income. It also helps you identify hidden expenses and risks that could otherwise erode your returns. This level of insight allows you to build a portfolio that is not only profitable on paper but also stable and resilient in real-world conditions.

Tenant selection and management is another critical component of successful rental investing, and AI plays a powerful role here as well. Poor tenant selection can turn a great investment into a stressful liability. With AI-driven screening tools and data analysis, you can better evaluate tenant reliability, payment history patterns, and behavioral indicators that reduce the risk of late payments or property damage. In addition, AI can help automate communication, maintenance tracking, and rent collection processes, making property management more efficient and less time-consuming.

This book also introduces the concept of portfolio strategy using AI. Instead of viewing rental properties as individual assets, you will learn how to think in terms of systems and portfolios. AI can help you analyze how each property contributes to your overall financial goals, identify gaps in your portfolio, and suggest acquisition strategies that align with your desired cash flow and equity growth. This allows you to move from random acquisitions to intentional portfolio building, where every property serves a specific purpose in your wealth strategy.

Another key advantage of AI in rental investing is market selection. Choosing the right market is often more important than choosing the right property. AI tools can analyze population growth, job trends, rental demand, price appreciation, and economic stability across multiple regions simultaneously. This gives you the ability to identify emerging markets before they become saturated, positioning you ahead of other investors who rely on traditional research methods. The result is better entry points, stronger cash flow, and higher long-term appreciation potential.

Throughout this book, you will also see how rental investing connects directly to financial independence. Unlike fix-and-flip strategies that generate one-time profits, rental properties create recurring monthly income that can eventually replace earned income entirely. AI accelerates this process by helping you scale faster, avoid costly mistakes, and reinvest profits more efficiently. Over time, this leads to a portfolio that not only generates income but also builds generational wealth.

As you move deeper into this book, you will begin to see rental investing not as a passive activity, but as an intelligently designed system powered by data, automation, and strategic decision-making. AI becomes your assistant in evaluating opportunities, managing risk, and optimizing performance. Instead of reacting to the market, you begin to anticipate it. Instead of guessing outcomes, you begin to calculate them.

By the end of this introduction, the foundation is clear: rental property investing is no longer about working harder or relying on experience alone. It is about using intelligent systems to make better decisions, faster decisions, and more profitable decisions. This is where AI transforms from a tool into a strategic advantage—one that allows you to build a rental portfolio designed not just for income today, but for freedom tomorrow.

Chapter 1

Understanding AI-Powered Rental & Cash Flow Investing Fundamentals

Rental property investing has always been one of the most stable and time-tested paths to building long-term wealth, but the way investors succeed in this space has changed dramatically. In the past, rental investing was driven heavily by experience, intuition, and local market knowledge. Investors would spend weeks analyzing neighborhoods, calling property managers, estimating rents manually, and relying on incomplete or outdated information. The result was often inconsistent performance—some investors succeeded, but many struggled with vacancies, unexpected expenses, poor tenant selection, and underperforming properties. Today, artificial intelligence is transforming this entire process by replacing guesswork with precision, speed, and data-driven decision-making.

At its core, AI-powered rental investing is about using intelligent systems to identify, evaluate, and manage income-producing properties with a level of efficiency that was previously impossible. Instead of manually gathering fragmented data from multiple sources, investors now have access to platforms that can analyze rental income potential, market demand, neighborhood trends, and property performance metrics in seconds. This shift allows investors to focus less on collecting information and more on making strategic decisions that build cash flow and long-term equity.

One of the most important concepts in rental investing is cash flow. Cash flow represents the income left over after all expenses are paid, including mortgage payments, taxes, insurance, maintenance, and property management. In traditional investing, calculating accurate cash flow required multiple assumptions and often led to unrealistic expectations. AI changes this by pulling real-time data from rental markets, comparable properties, and historical performance trends to create highly accurate projections. This allows investors to clearly understand whether a property will generate positive or negative monthly income before they ever make an offer.

Another major transformation AI brings to rental investing is market selection. Choosing the right market is often more important than choosing the right property. A great property in a declining market will underperform, while an average property in a high-demand market can generate strong, consistent returns. AI tools can analyze population growth, employment trends, rental demand, school ratings, crime statistics, and economic indicators across entire regions simultaneously. This gives investors the ability to identify high-growth rental markets early, often before they become competitive or overpriced.

In addition to market selection, AI also enhances property selection within those markets. Investors can quickly compare dozens or even hundreds of properties based on key financial metrics such as cap rate, cash-on-cash return, price-to-rent ratio, and projected appreciation. Instead of relying on emotional decision-making or surface-level comparisons, investors can now filter opportunities based on strict investment criteria. This reduces the likelihood of making poor purchasing decisions and increases the probability of building a profitable portfolio.

Tenant screening is another area where AI is creating significant improvements. Traditionally, tenant selection relied heavily on credit reports, income verification, and references. While these factors are still important, AI adds another layer of predictive analysis. It can identify patterns in tenant behavior, assess risk levels based on historical data, and flag potential issues before they become problems. This reduces the risk of late payments, evictions, and property damage, which are some of the biggest threats to rental profitability.

Property management is also becoming more automated through AI systems. Tasks such as rent collection, maintenance scheduling, tenant communication, and financial reporting can now be handled through intelligent platforms. This reduces the time burden on investors and allows them to scale their portfolios without becoming overwhelmed by day-to-day operations. Instead of managing every detail manually, investors can oversee systems that run in the background and provide real-time updates on performance.

Another key advantage of AI in rental investing is risk management. Every investment carries risk, but AI helps quantify and minimize that risk by analyzing multiple variables simultaneously. It can identify properties with high maintenance costs, unstable rental demand, or declining neighborhood conditions. It can also simulate different scenarios, such as interest rate changes or vacancy fluctuations, to show how a property will perform under different conditions. This allows investors to prepare for uncertainty rather than react to it.

As investors begin to integrate AI into their rental strategies, the entire approach to wealth building changes. Instead of focusing on individual deals, investors begin to think in terms of systems and portfolios. Each property becomes part of a larger income strategy designed to produce consistent cash flow and long-term appreciation. AI helps connect these individual investments into a cohesive portfolio that is optimized for performance, scalability, and financial independence.

Ultimately, the fundamentals of rental investing have not changed—but the tools have. Cash flow is still the goal. Good tenants are still essential. Strong markets still matter. What has changed is the level of intelligence and precision available to investors. AI does not replace the investor; it enhances the investor's ability to make better decisions faster and with far less risk. Those who learn to integrate these tools into their strategy gain a significant advantage in building wealth through real estate.

This chapter sets the foundation for everything that follows. In the next sections, we will go deeper into how AI identifies profitable rental opportunities, optimizes pricing strategies, improves tenant selection, and ultimately builds scalable cash-flowing portfolios that generate income long after the initial investment is made.

"The Shift From Landlord to System Builder"

Ethan had always believed rental real estate was supposed to be simple. Buy a property, rent it out, collect monthly income, and repeat. That was the plan he had heard from countless investors, podcasts, and seminars. But reality had been far more complicated. His first property looked perfect on paper. The numbers made sense, the neighborhood seemed stable, and the rent projections were promising. But within months, things began to fall apart. The tenant missed payments, unexpected repairs drained his savings, and what was supposed to be passive income turned into constant stress.

For years, Ethan tried to fix the problem by working harder. He studied market reports, talked to property managers, and even attended local real estate meetups. Still, nothing felt consistent. Some properties performed well, others barely broke even, and a few became financial burdens. He started to question whether rental investing was truly the path to financial freedom or just another demanding job in disguise.

Everything changed the day he was introduced to AI-based rental analysis tools. At first, he was skeptical. The idea that a system could evaluate rental properties better than his own experience felt unrealistic. But curiosity pushed him forward. He entered one of his potential deals into an AI platform. Within seconds, the system generated a full breakdown—cash flow projections, neighborhood demand analysis, risk assessment, tenant stability indicators, and even long-term appreciation forecasts.

What shocked him most was not just the speed, but the accuracy. The AI identified hidden risks in the property he had completely overlooked, including rising maintenance costs in the area and declining rental demand in a nearby segment of the neighborhood. It also highlighted a different property nearby that had stronger cash flow potential, better tenant demographics, and lower long-term risk.

For the first time, Ethan realized that he had been making decisions with incomplete information. He wasn't investing wrong—he was simply investing blind.

He began using AI for every part of his process. Instead of spending weeks researching markets, he could now compare entire cities in minutes. Instead of guessing rental prices, he had real-time data. Instead of hoping tenants would be reliable, he had predictive insights into tenant behavior. Slowly, his approach to investing began to change.

But the biggest shift was not in his tools—it was in his mindset. Ethan stopped thinking like a landlord and started thinking like a system builder. He no longer focused on individual properties as isolated investments. Instead, he began building a portfolio designed with intention. Each property had a role: some for stable cash flow, others for long-term appreciation, and a few positioned for equity growth.

As his portfolio grew, so did his confidence. Vacancies became rare. Cash flow became predictable. Stress began to fade. For the first time, rental investing felt structured instead of chaotic.

One evening, as he reviewed his portfolio dashboard, Ethan noticed something powerful. His properties were now generating more monthly income than his primary job. But more importantly, they were doing it without his constant involvement. AI systems were handling tenant screening, maintenance alerts, rent tracking, and financial reporting.

He leaned back and realized something that had taken him years to understand. He had not become a better landlord by working harder. He had become a better investor by building a better system.

And that system—powered by AI—was just getting started.

Chapter 2

AI Market Selection and Finding High-Cash-Flow Rental Opportunities

One of the most critical decisions in rental property investing is not the property itself, but the market in which that property exists. Many investors focus heavily on analyzing individual homes, yet the reality is that even a great property can underperform in a weak or declining market. Conversely, an average property in a strong rental market can generate consistent cash flow, long-term appreciation, and lower risk. This is where artificial intelligence becomes a game-changing advantage, because it allows investors to evaluate entire markets with a level of speed, depth, and accuracy that was previously impossible.

Traditionally, market selection required months of research, travel, and local networking. Investors would rely on anecdotal information, outdated reports, and limited data points such as median home prices or average rent levels. This approach often led to emotional decision-making and missed opportunities in emerging markets. AI transforms this process by analyzing massive datasets across multiple cities and regions simultaneously. It evaluates job growth, population migration patterns, rental demand, income levels, housing supply, and economic stability in real time, allowing investors to identify high-performing markets before they become widely recognized.

At the core of AI-driven market selection is data aggregation. AI systems pull information from public records, rental platforms, economic databases, and real estate listing services to create a complete picture of a market's performance. Instead of looking at one or two indicators, investors can now see a full ecosystem of factors that influence rental success. This includes vacancy rates, average days on market, rent-to-price ratios, and historical appreciation trends. When combined, these insights allow for far more accurate forecasting of future performance.

One of the most powerful advantages of AI in market selection is its ability to identify emerging markets early. These are areas where growth is beginning but has not yet reached mainstream attention. For example, a city experiencing new job growth from tech companies, infrastructure expansion, or population migration may show strong rental potential long before prices rise significantly. AI can detect these early signals by analyzing patterns across multiple data sources, giving investors a first-mover advantage that can dramatically increase long-term returns. Once a market is identified, AI helps narrow the focus to specific neighborhoods and zip codes. Not all areas within a strong city perform equally. Some neighborhoods may have high demand but limited supply, while others may have rising crime rates or stagnant rental growth. AI tools break markets down into micro-segments, allowing investors to compare neighborhoods based on rental yield, tenant demographics, school ratings, and local economic activity. This level of precision helps investors avoid weak pockets within otherwise strong markets.

Another key element of AI market selection is rental demand forecasting. Understanding whether tenants will consistently want to live in a specific area is essential for long-term success. AI models analyze rental search trends, population density changes, employment hubs, and housing affordability metrics to predict future demand. This allows investors to position themselves in areas where demand is likely to increase rather than decline, reducing vacancy risk and improving cash flow stability.

AI also plays a major role in pricing strategy and rent optimization. Even after selecting the right market, setting the correct rental price is critical. Overpricing can lead to long vacancies, while underpricing reduces profitability. AI tools compare similar rental properties in real time and adjust pricing recommendations based on current market conditions. This ensures that investors maximize income while remaining competitive within the market.

Risk assessment is another essential component of AI-powered market selection. Every market carries different levels of risk based on economic stability, employment diversity, and housing supply. AI evaluates these risk factors simultaneously and assigns predictive scores to help investors understand the potential volatility of each market. This allows for more balanced portfolio construction, where high-growth markets can be paired with stable, low-risk areas to create consistent cash flow.

Financing considerations are also influenced by market selection. Lenders often evaluate risk based on location, property type, and rental demand. AI helps investors identify markets that not only perform well in terms of cash flow but also meet lending criteria for DSCR loans and other investment financing options. This increases the likelihood of approval and improves loan terms, which directly impacts overall returns.

Ultimately, AI-driven market selection transforms rental investing from a reactive process into a proactive strategy. Instead of chasing deals in familiar areas, investors can now systematically scan the entire country for high-performing opportunities. This expands the playing field and removes geographic limitations that once restricted growth. Investors are no longer tied to their local markets—they can operate nationally with data-driven confidence.

As this chapter progresses, the focus will shift from identifying strong markets to selecting individual properties within those markets using AI-powered filters and evaluation systems. This next stage is where opportunity becomes actionable, and where data begins to turn into real cash flow.

"The Market That Everyone Else Missed"

When Daniel first started investing in rental properties, he did what most beginners did. He focused on his local market. It felt safe, familiar, and easy to understand. He knew the neighborhoods, he understood the pricing, and he believed that staying close to home would reduce risk. His first few deals were average at best. Some cash flowed slightly, others barely broke even, and a few required constant repairs that drained his profits.

For a while, Daniel assumed this was just how rental investing worked. Slow growth, small wins, and occasional setbacks. But everything changed when he saw another investor posting results online that seemed almost unreal. This investor was buying properties in cities Daniel had never even considered, yet the returns were significantly higher, and the cash flow was consistent month after month.

Curious, Daniel began researching these markets manually. He spent hours reading reports, comparing rent prices, and analyzing listings. But the process felt overwhelming and incomplete. There were too many variables, too much scattered information, and no clear way to determine which markets were actually worth entering.

That's when he discovered AI-powered market analysis tools.

At first, he treated it like a test. He entered a few cities he was curious about into the system and waited for the results. Within moments, he saw something he had never seen before—clear rankings of markets based on rental demand, cash flow potential, job growth, population trends, and risk factors. Instead of guessing, he was looking at structured intelligence.

One market stood out immediately. It was not a major city, not a well-known investment hub, and not a place most investors talked about. In fact, Daniel had barely considered it before. But the AI analysis showed something different. Strong population growth, rising rental demand, affordable entry prices, and a growing job market fueled by new infrastructure development.

Skeptical but intrigued, Daniel dug deeper. The numbers were consistent across multiple datasets. Vacancy rates were low. Rent prices were increasing steadily. And most importantly, property prices were still undervalued compared to similar markets.

For the first time, Daniel realized he had been investing based on familiarity rather than opportunity.

He decided to take action.

Within weeks, he acquired his first property in the new market. The process was smoother than expected because he had already validated the area through AI data. Financing was approved quickly, tenants were secured faster than in his local market, and cash flow exceeded his previous investments.

Encouraged by the results, Daniel expanded further. Each new property followed the same system: AI market analysis first, then neighborhood selection, then property acquisition. The emotional stress he once felt began to disappear, replaced by structured decision-making and predictable outcomes.

Over time, something remarkable happened. His portfolio stopped being dependent on chance. He was no longer hoping a market would perform well—he was selecting markets that were statistically designed for performance.

One evening, while reviewing his portfolio dashboard, Daniel noticed something striking. The majority of his income was now coming from markets he had never physically visited before. Places he once ignored were now the foundation of his financial stability.

He leaned back and thought about how different things used to be. He used to rely on gut feeling, local advice, and limited knowledge. Now he relied on systems that analyzed entire economies in seconds.

And in that moment, Daniel understood the real shift.

He was no longer a local investor making scattered decisions.

He was a data-driven investor operating in markets chosen by intelligence—not instinct.

And that changed everything.

Chapter 3

AI Property Selection and Cash Flow Optimization in Rental Investing

Once a strong rental market has been identified, the next and most critical step in building a profitable portfolio is selecting the right properties within that market. This is where many investors either accelerate their success or unknowingly sabotage it. A strong market does not guarantee strong performance unless the individual property is aligned with cash flow goals, rental demand, and long-term financial strategy. Artificial intelligence transforms this stage by removing emotional decision-making and replacing it with structured, data-driven property evaluation.

In traditional investing, property selection often relied on surface-level analysis. Investors would look at listing photos, compare asking prices, estimate rent based on nearby properties, and make assumptions about future value. This approach created significant risk because it lacked precision and failed to account for hidden costs, market fluctuations, and tenant behavior. AI changes this entirely by analyzing hundreds of variables simultaneously, including rental demand, neighborhood trends, property condition indicators, historical appreciation, and projected maintenance costs.

One of the most powerful capabilities of AI in property selection is its ability to calculate true cash flow with accuracy. Cash flow is not just rent minus mortgage—it is a complex equation that includes taxes, insurance, maintenance reserves, vacancy rates, property management fees, and unexpected repairs. AI systems integrate all of these variables into a single model that shows investors a realistic monthly and annual profit projection. This eliminates guesswork and helps investors avoid properties that appear profitable on paper but fail in real-world conditions.

Another major advantage of AI is its ability to compare multiple properties instantly. Instead of analyzing one deal at a time, investors can input dozens of properties and receive ranked recommendations based on performance metrics. These rankings often include cash-on-cash return, cap rate, rental yield, appreciation potential, and risk score. This allows investors to focus only on the highest-performing opportunities instead of wasting time on marginal deals.

AI also enhances rental pricing strategy, which is essential for maximizing cash flow. Setting the correct rent is one of the most important factors in long-term success. If rent is set too high, vacancies increase. If it is set too low, income potential is lost. AI tools analyze real-time rental listings, tenant demand trends, seasonal fluctuations, and neighborhood competition to recommend optimal pricing strategies. This ensures that properties remain both competitive and profitable.

Another key feature of AI property analysis is risk detection. Every property carries hidden risks that may not be obvious during initial evaluation. These can include high maintenance neighborhoods, aging infrastructure, tenant turnover rates, or declining demand trends. AI systems flag these risks early, allowing investors to either renegotiate purchase prices or avoid problematic deals entirely. This reduces costly surprises after acquisition.

Tenant demand prediction is another critical element of AI-powered property selection. Even a well-priced property in a strong location can struggle if tenant demand is weak. AI evaluates demographic trends, employment centers, school districts, and lifestyle preferences to predict how quickly a property will rent and how stable tenants are likely to be. This helps investors prioritize properties that not only generate income but also maintain occupancy stability.

Financing optimization is also influenced by AI property selection. Different properties qualify for different loan products, including DSCR loans, conventional financing, and alternative lending structures. AI can simulate how each financing option impacts monthly cash flow and long-term returns. This allows investors to structure deals in a way that maximizes profitability while minimizing financial strain.

One of the most overlooked advantages of AI in property selection is its ability to model long-term performance. Many investors focus only on immediate cash flow, but true wealth in rental investing comes from long-term appreciation combined with sustained income. AI tools simulate property performance over 5, 10, and even 20-year periods, showing how equity growth, rent increases, and market appreciation will impact total returns. This shifts decision-making from short-term thinking to long-term wealth building.

AI also helps investors avoid emotional traps. It is easy to fall in love with a property based on appearance, location appeal, or personal preference. However, emotional decisions often lead to poor investment outcomes. AI removes emotion from the equation by focusing strictly on data. A beautiful property that performs poorly financially is rejected, while a less attractive property with strong cash flow is prioritized. As investors begin to rely more heavily on AI for property selection, their portfolios become more consistent and predictable. Instead of experiencing random success and failure, each acquisition follows a structured system designed to maximize return and minimize risk. Over time, this leads to stronger cash flow, lower vacancy rates, and more efficient portfolio scaling.

Ultimately, AI property selection is about precision. It allows investors to move beyond assumptions and into a world where every decision is backed by data. This creates a level of confidence that traditional investing methods cannot match. The result is not just better properties—it is better portfolios, better income stability, and a clearer path toward financial independence.

In the next chapter, we will explore how AI transforms tenant screening, property management, and long-term portfolio optimization, turning rental investing into a fully automated wealth-building system.

"The Property That Should Have Failed—but Didn't"

Marcus had always believed he had a good eye for real estate. He could walk through a property and instantly get a "feel" for whether it was a good deal or not. For years, that intuition had served him reasonably well—at least, that's what he thought. Some properties performed, others struggled, and a few turned into expensive lessons. But overall, he assumed experience was enough to guide his decisions.

That changed the day he met an investor who didn't talk about intuition at all. Instead, this investor talked about data, models, and AI-driven property analysis. Marcus was skeptical. Real estate, in his mind, was still a relationship and experience business. But curiosity pushed him to look deeper.

He decided to test an AI property analysis tool on a deal he was currently considering.

On the surface, the property looked promising. It was in a decent neighborhood, had a fair asking price, and appeared to rent easily based on nearby listings. Marcus had already run rough calculations and believed it could produce solid cash flow. He was close to making an offer.

Before committing, he entered the property into the AI system.

Within seconds, everything changed.

The system didn't just give him a yes or no. It gave him a complete breakdown. Cash flow projections were lower than expected. Maintenance costs were higher than similar properties in the area. Vacancy risk was elevated due to shifting tenant demographics. And most importantly, the long-term appreciation potential was weaker than comparable neighborhoods just a few miles away.

Marcus was surprised. On paper, everything had looked fine. But the AI analysis revealed hidden weaknesses he had completely missed.

Out of curiosity, he decided to compare the property with others in the same market. The AI instantly generated a ranked list of better-performing properties. One stood out immediately. It was slightly less attractive visually, located in a less "popular" street, but the financial metrics were significantly stronger. Higher cash flow, lower maintenance risk, better tenant stability, and stronger long-term appreciation potential.

Marcus hesitated. His instinct was still pulling him toward the original property. It looked better. It felt more familiar. But the data was clear.

He decided to trust the system.

He made an offer on the AI-recommended property instead.

Within weeks of closing, the difference became obvious. The

property rented faster than expected. Maintenance issues were minimal. Cash flow was consistent and higher than his previous investments. For the first time, Marcus didn't feel like he was managing uncertainty—he felt like he was managing performance.

Meanwhile, the property he almost purchased went under contract with another investor. Curious, Marcus kept track of it. Within months, that investor began facing issues—long vacancies, unexpected repairs, and lower-than-expected rent. It was performing exactly as the AI had predicted.

That moment changed Marcus's entire approach.

He stopped relying on instinct.

He stopped trusting "feel."

Instead, he began using AI as the foundation of every property decision.

Over time, his portfolio transformed. Each new acquisition followed a strict data-driven process. Properties were no longer chosen because they looked good or felt right—they were chosen because they performed well under analysis.

His income stabilized. His stress decreased. And his

confidence in investing reached a level he had never experienced before. One evening, while reviewing his portfolio dashboard, Marcus noticed something that made him pause. Every single property he owned had been selected or validated by AI. And every one of them was outperforming his earlier investments.

He leaned back and realized something simple but powerful.

He hadn't become a better investor by trusting his instincts more.

He had become a better investor by replacing instincts with intelligence.

And that shift had changed everything.

Chapter 4

AI Tenant Screening, Rent Optimization, and Automated Property Management Systems

As rental property investing evolves, one of the most overlooked yet most critical components of long-term success is not acquiring the property itself, but managing it effectively once it is occupied. Many investors focus heavily on acquisition strategies, market selection, and cash flow projections, but fail to fully optimize what happens after the tenant moves in. This is where real profitability is either sustained or slowly eroded. Artificial intelligence now plays a central role in transforming property management from a reactive, stressful process into a proactive, automated system that protects income, reduces risk, and improves tenant quality over time.

Tenant screening has traditionally been one of the most subjective parts of rental investing. Investors relied on credit scores, income verification, rental history, and references. While these are still important, they do not always reveal the full picture of tenant behavior. A tenant with good credit can still create payment delays, property damage, or communication issues. AI enhances tenant screening by analyzing behavioral patterns, payment consistency trends, employment stability indicators, and historical rental behavior models. This allows investors to move beyond surface-level qualifications and evaluate deeper risk profiles.

AI-driven tenant screening systems aggregate data from multiple sources to create a more complete tenant risk assessment. Instead of simply approving or rejecting applicants based on static criteria, AI evaluates likelihood of late payments, lease violations, and early lease termination. This predictive capability helps investors select tenants who are more likely to remain stable and reliable over time, reducing turnover and vacancy costs. The result is a more consistent income stream and fewer disruptions to cash flow.

Once a tenant is placed, AI continues to play a role in rent optimization. Setting the correct rent is one of the most important decisions in maintaining profitability. Many landlords either underprice their rentals, leaving money on the table, or overprice them, leading to longer vacancies. AI solves this problem by continuously analyzing local rental listings, demand shifts, seasonal trends, and competitor pricing. It provides real-time recommendations for optimal rent pricing that balances occupancy speed with maximum income.

Rent optimization is not a one-time decision. Markets change constantly due to economic shifts, interest rates, job growth, and population movement. AI systems continuously monitor these changes and recommend adjustments when necessary. This ensures that rental properties remain competitively priced without sacrificing long-term income potential. Over time, this dynamic pricing strategy can significantly increase total annual returns across a portfolio.

Another major transformation AI brings to rental investing is automated property management. Traditionally, property management required constant human involvement—handling maintenance requests, communicating with tenants, tracking payments, coordinating repairs, and managing documentation. These tasks are time-consuming and difficult to scale. AI-powered systems now automate many of these responsibilities through integrated platforms that handle communication, scheduling, and financial tracking.

For example, when a tenant submits a maintenance request, AI can categorize the issue, prioritize urgency, and automatically assign it to the appropriate vendor. It can also track response times, estimate repair costs, and provide real-time updates to both tenant and owner. This eliminates delays, reduces miscommunication, and improves tenant satisfaction. In many cases, issues are resolved faster and more efficiently than traditional property management methods.

AI also improves rent collection efficiency. Automated systems can send reminders, process payments, track late fees, and escalate issues when necessary. This reduces the likelihood of missed payments and improves overall cash flow consistency. For investors managing multiple properties, this automation is essential for scalability, as it eliminates the need for constant manual follow-up.

Another important component of AI property management is financial tracking and reporting. Investors need clear visibility into income, expenses, cash flow, and overall portfolio performance. AI systems consolidate financial data from multiple properties and generate real-time dashboards that show profitability trends, expense breakdowns, and performance comparisons. This allows investors to make informed decisions quickly without waiting for monthly reports or manual calculations.

Maintenance prediction is another powerful feature of AI in property management. Instead of reacting to repairs after they occur, AI can analyze property age, usage patterns, and historical maintenance data to predict when systems are likely to fail. This allows investors to proactively address issues before they become expensive emergencies. Over time, this reduces maintenance costs and extends the lifespan of property systems.

Tenant communication is also significantly improved through AI automation. Chatbots and automated messaging systems can handle routine inquiries, provide updates, and manage basic requests without human intervention. This ensures that tenants receive fast responses while freeing up investors or property managers to focus on higher-level decision-making. Improved communication leads to higher tenant satisfaction and longer lease durations.

Portfolio scalability is one of the most important outcomes of AI-powered property management. Without automation, managing multiple properties becomes overwhelming. With AI, investors can scale their portfolios without increasing operational stress. Systems handle repetitive tasks, monitor performance, and alert investors only when strategic decisions are required. This allows rental investing to shift from an active job into a semi-passive or fully passive income system.

Ultimately, AI tenant screening, rent optimization, and property management work together to create a complete ecosystem of efficiency and control. Each component reinforces the others—better tenants reduce maintenance issues, optimized rent improves cash flow, and automation reduces operational workload. The result is a rental portfolio that is not only profitable but also stable and scalable.

In the next chapter, we will explore how AI is used to build fully optimized rental portfolios, connect multiple properties into a unified financial system, and prepare investors for long-term wealth scaling and financial independence.

"The Portfolio That Ran Without Chaos"

Samantha remembered the early days of her rental investing journey as overwhelming and chaotic. She had worked hard to acquire her first few properties, but managing them quickly became more stressful than she expected. Tenant calls came at inconvenient hours, maintenance issues piled up unexpectedly, and rent payments were inconsistent. She found herself constantly reacting to problems instead of building wealth.

At first, she believed this was just part of being a landlord. Everyone told her that rental income was "passive," but her experience felt anything but passive. It felt like another full-time job. She was managing repairs, chasing payments, screening tenants, and trying to keep everything organized manually. Despite owning properties, she rarely felt in control.

One evening, after dealing with yet another late-night maintenance issue, Samantha reached a breaking point. She began searching for ways to simplify her process and discovered AI-powered property management systems. Initially, she was skeptical. The idea that software could manage tenants, rent collection, and maintenance felt unrealistic. But she was willing to try anything that could reduce stress.

She started by integrating AI tenant screening into her leasing process. Instead of relying solely on credit scores and applications, she allowed the system to analyze deeper behavioral patterns and risk indicators. The difference was immediate. The quality of tenants improved. Fewer late payments. Fewer disputes. More stable occupancy.

Encouraged, she moved to rent optimization tools. One of her properties had been underperforming for months. She had assumed the rent was set correctly because it matched nearby listings. But AI analysis showed she was significantly underpriced based on demand trends and neighborhood growth. After adjusting the rent slightly, she not only increased monthly income but still maintained full occupancy.

That was the moment she realized something important. She had been guessing, not optimizing.

Next came automation. She connected her properties to an AI property management system. Suddenly, everything changed. Maintenance requests were categorized automatically. Vendors were assigned without delay. Rent reminders were sent without her involvement. Payments were tracked and recorded in real time. For the first time, she was no longer managing chaos—she was overseeing a system.

At first, she didn't fully trust it. She still checked everything manually. But over time, she noticed something surprising. The system was not only consistent—it was better than her manual management. Fewer errors. Faster response times. Happier tenants.

Months passed, and Samantha began to step back from day-to-day involvement. Instead of reacting to problems, she started reviewing reports. Instead of chasing rent, she watched automated systems handle it. Instead of coordinating repairs, she saw them scheduled and completed without her input.

One day, she took a trip and decided not to check her properties for an entire week. It was the first time she had ever done that. She expected issues when she returned. But when she opened her dashboard, everything was normal.

Rent had been collected. Maintenance requests had been resolved. Tenants were satisfied. Cash flow was stable.

Nothing had broken.

In fact, everything had improved.

Samantha sat quietly, realizing something she had never experienced before.

Her rental properties were no longer dependent on her constant attention.

They were running as a system.

And that system—powered by AI—was more stable than anything she had ever built on her own.

Chapter 5

AI Portfolio Strategy, Scaling Rental Income, and Building Long-Term Wealth Systems

As investors move beyond acquiring and managing individual rental properties, the next stage of wealth creation is understanding how to build a cohesive portfolio that functions as a unified financial system. This is where true financial independence begins to take shape. Owning properties is not enough on its own; the real power comes from how those properties interact, perform, and scale together over time. Artificial intelligence plays a transformative role in this stage by allowing investors to design, optimize, and expand entire rental portfolios based on data-driven strategy rather than random acquisition.

A rental portfolio is more than a collection of properties. It is a structured system designed to produce consistent cash flow, long-term appreciation, and risk-balanced income streams. Traditionally, investors built portfolios reactively, purchasing properties when opportunities arose without a larger strategic framework. This often resulted in uneven cash flow, geographic concentration risk, and inconsistent performance. AI changes this by enabling investors to model entire portfolios before they are built, simulating how each property contributes to overall income, risk exposure, and long-term wealth growth.

One of the most powerful capabilities of AI in portfolio strategy is predictive modeling. Instead of analyzing properties individually, AI systems can project how multiple assets will perform together under different economic conditions. This includes interest rate changes, rental demand fluctuations, vacancy cycles, and market appreciation scenarios. By simulating these conditions, investors can build portfolios that remain stable even in uncertain markets. This transforms rental investing from a reactive process into a forward-looking strategy.

AI also helps investors balance their portfolios across multiple dimensions. A strong rental portfolio is not just about maximizing cash flow—it is about balancing stability, growth, and liquidity. Some properties may generate high monthly income but slower appreciation, while others may offer strong long-term equity growth but moderate cash flow. AI helps investors identify the optimal mix of property types, locations, and financing structures to achieve a balanced and resilient portfolio. Another critical aspect of portfolio scaling is acquisition sequencing. The order in which properties are acquired can significantly impact financial outcomes. AI tools can analyze financing capacity, market timing, interest rate environments, and cash flow accumulation to recommend the most strategic acquisition path. This ensures that each new property strengthens the portfolio rather than creating financial strain. Investors can scale more efficiently without overleveraging or compromising cash flow stability.

AI also plays a major role in capital recycling strategies. As properties appreciate or generate equity, investors often refinance or sell assets to reinvest capital into new opportunities. AI systems can identify the optimal timing for refinancing or selling based on market conditions, interest rate trends, and portfolio performance. This allows investors to continuously grow their portfolio without relying solely on external capital.

Risk diversification is another essential element of portfolio strategy. Concentrating investments in one geographic area or property type can expose investors to unnecessary risk. AI analyzes geographic, economic, and tenant-related risk factors to ensure diversification across markets and property classes.

This reduces vulnerability to localized downturns and improves long-term income stability.

AI also enhances long-term forecasting, which is essential for wealth planning. Instead of focusing only on monthly cash flow, investors can now project 10-, 15-, or 20-year portfolio performance. These forecasts include rent growth projections, property appreciation, mortgage payoff timelines, and equity accumulation. This level of insight allows investors to make decisions based on lifetime wealth creation rather than short-term gains.

Another important feature of AI portfolio management is performance optimization. Over time, not all properties perform equally. AI identifies underperforming assets within a portfolio and suggests corrective actions such as rent adjustments, refinancing, selling, or repositioning. This ensures that the portfolio remains optimized at all times rather than becoming stagnant or inefficient.

Automation also plays a key role in scaling portfolios. As the number of properties increases, manual management becomes impossible. AI systems handle rent tracking, maintenance coordination, financial reporting, tenant communication, and performance monitoring. This allows investors to scale from a few properties to dozens or even hundreds without increasing operational complexity. Ultimately, AI portfolio strategy transforms rental investing into a structured wealth-building system. Instead of relying on isolated decisions, investors operate within a connected ecosystem where every property serves a purpose. Cash flow becomes predictable, risk becomes manageable, and growth becomes intentional. This is the point where rental investing evolves from a side strategy into a full financial infrastructure.

In the next chapter, we will explore how AI integrates financing strategies, DSCR loans, leverage optimization, and capital structuring to accelerate portfolio growth and unlock even greater levels of scalability and financial control.

"The Portfolio That Became a Machine"

Michael never intended to become a large-scale real estate investor. At first, he simply wanted a few rental properties to supplement his income. His goal was modest—replace a portion of his salary and build some long-term security for his family. He started with one property, then another, and slowly over time, his portfolio grew. But growth came with complexity.

At five properties, things were manageable. At ten, things

became complicated. At fifteen, everything started to feel disconnected. Some properties performed well, others underperformed, and he had no clear system to understand why. Cash flow fluctuated unpredictably, and managing everything felt like juggling multiple separate businesses.

Michael realized he didn't have a portfolio. He had a collection of independent investments.

That realization frustrated him because despite working harder, he didn't feel closer to financial freedom. Instead, he felt more overwhelmed. Each property required attention, and every decision felt reactive rather than strategic.

One day, while researching ways to improve his system, he discovered AI portfolio management tools. Unlike the property-level tools he had used before, this system analyzed his entire portfolio as one interconnected structure. It showed him cash flow distribution, risk exposure, geographic concentration, and long-term performance projections.

For the first time, Michael could see his entire financial ecosystem in one place.

What he saw surprised him.

Some properties were carrying the portfolio while others were dragging it down. A few properties had strong appreciation potential but weak cash flow, while others generated income but offered no long-term growth. There was no balance, no structure, no intentional design.

He had been building randomly.

Using AI recommendations, Michael began restructuring his portfolio. He identified underperforming properties and refinanced two of them to improve cash flow. He sold another that had stagnant growth and reinvested the equity into a stronger market identified by the system. For the first time, every decision was intentional.

As he continued, something began to change. His portfolio stopped feeling like separate properties and started functioning like a single system. AI provided acquisition recommendations based on gaps in his portfolio. If he lacked cash-flow-heavy assets, it suggested those. If he lacked appreciation-focused properties, it identified markets that filled that gap.

Over time, Michael stopped thinking in terms of individual deals. He started thinking in terms of portfolio performance.

Months passed, and the transformation became undeniable. His income stabilized. His growth accelerated. And most importantly, his stress decreased. He no longer worried about which property needed attention that day. Instead, he focused on high-level decisions while the system handled execution. One evening, Michael opened his portfolio dashboard and noticed something that made him pause. His properties were no longer listed as separate investments. They were displayed as a unified system—showing total income, total equity, projected growth, and risk balance.

It didn't look like a list anymore.

It looked like a machine.

A system that produced income, managed risk, and expanded wealth automatically.

Michael leaned back and realized something profound.

He had not just built a portfolio.

He had built a financial engine.

And for the first time, that engine was no longer dependent on constant effort—it was powered by structure, intelligence, and systems that worked even when he wasn't watching.

Chapter 6

AI Scaling Strategies, Leverage, and Building a Self-Expanding Rental Empire

Once a rental portfolio reaches a level of stability and consistent cash flow, the next stage of wealth creation is scaling. Scaling is where most investors either accelerate toward financial freedom or become stuck in a plateau of limited growth. The difference between these outcomes often comes down to how effectively leverage, systems, and strategic expansion are used. Artificial intelligence fundamentally transforms this stage by allowing investors to scale with precision, speed, and control rather than risk and speculation.

In traditional real estate investing, scaling was heavily dependent on manual processes. Investors had to continuously search for deals, evaluate financing options, manage lenders, and coordinate acquisitions one by one. Growth was linear and slow. Each new property added complexity and required additional time and effort. AI changes this dynamic by automating deal sourcing, financing analysis, and portfolio impact evaluation, allowing investors to scale exponentially rather than incrementally.

One of the most powerful scaling tools in rental investing is leverage. Leverage allows investors to use borrowed capital to acquire income-producing assets that generate returns greater than the cost of debt. However, improper use of leverage can increase risk and destabilize a portfolio. AI helps optimize leverage by analyzing debt-to-income ratios, cash flow coverage, interest rate environments, and lender requirements to determine the safest and most profitable financing structure for each acquisition.

AI also plays a critical role in DSCR-based lending strategies, where loan qualification is based on property income rather than personal income. This is especially important for scaling because it allows investors to acquire multiple properties without being limited by personal financial documentation. AI tools can simulate DSCR ratios, predict lender approval likelihood, and identify the most favorable financing structures based on current market conditions.

Another key scaling strategy is capital recycling. As properties generate equity through appreciation and mortgage paydown, investors can refinance or sell assets to unlock capital for new acquisitions. AI systems analyze timing windows for refinancing based on interest rates, equity growth, and market cycles. This ensures that capital is recycled efficiently and reinvested into higher-performing opportunities without unnecessary delays or financial strain.

AI also enables investors to identify portfolio inefficiencies that limit scaling potential. For example, a property that produces moderate cash flow but ties up significant capital may be flagged for repositioning. Similarly, underperforming assets can be identified and replaced with higher-yield investments. This continuous optimization process ensures that capital is always allocated to its highest and best use within the portfolio.

A major barrier to scaling is operational complexity. As portfolios grow, management becomes increasingly difficult without systems in place. AI solves this by automating property management functions such as rent collection, maintenance coordination, tenant communication, and financial reporting. This reduces the need for manual oversight and allows investors to focus on strategic expansion rather than daily operations.

AI also enhances deal flow efficiency by continuously scanning markets for new opportunities that align with portfolio goals.

Instead of manually searching for properties, investors receive data-driven recommendations based on cash flow targets, risk tolerance, and portfolio gaps. This turns deal sourcing into a passive, automated process that operates in the background while the investor focuses on decision-making.

Risk management becomes even more important during scaling. As portfolios expand, exposure to market fluctuations increases. AI helps mitigate this risk by modeling worst-case scenarios, stress-testing portfolios against economic downturns, and identifying vulnerabilities in geographic or asset-class concentration. This allows investors to scale aggressively while maintaining structural stability.

Another critical aspect of scaling is timing. Expanding too quickly can lead to overleveraging and cash flow instability, while expanding too slowly can result in missed opportunities. AI analyzes market cycles, financing conditions, and portfolio performance to recommend optimal scaling pace. This ensures that growth is both sustainable and strategically timed.

Ultimately, AI transforms scaling from a high-risk expansion strategy into a controlled, system-driven process. Investors are no longer limited by time, geography, or manual workload. Instead, they operate within an intelligent ecosystem that continuously identifies opportunities, optimizes capital allocation, and manages risk in real time. In the next chapter, we will explore how AI integrates all components of rental investing into a fully automated ecosystem—where acquisitions, management, financing, and scaling operate together as a single self-sustaining wealth engine.

"The Moment the Portfolio Outgrew the Investor"

Jason always believed that scaling a real estate portfolio was supposed to feel exciting. More properties meant more income, more freedom, and more success. But what he experienced was something very different. As his portfolio grew from three properties to eight, and then to twelve, the excitement turned into pressure. Every new acquisition added complexity. Every property added responsibilities. And instead of feeling more free, Jason felt more trapped.

He was constantly analyzing deals, checking rent payments, coordinating repairs, and communicating with tenants. Even when properties were performing well, the workload never stopped. He realized that he was not building a passive income system—he was building a management burden.

One night, after spending hours trying to decide whether to acquire his next property, Jason stumbled across an AI scaling system designed for rental portfolios. At first, he almost ignored it. He assumed it would be just another analysis tool. But what caught his attention was something different. This system didn't just evaluate properties—it evaluated entire portfolios and recommended scaling strategies.

Curious, Jason connected his portfolio to the system.

Within minutes, everything changed.

The AI didn't just show him what he owned. It showed him how everything was performing together. Some properties were driving most of his cash flow, while others were barely breaking even. More importantly, it showed him that his portfolio was becoming unbalanced. He had too many moderate-cash-flow properties and not enough high-growth assets to sustain long-term scaling.

Then the system did something he didn't expect. It began recommending actions.

Refinance this property to release equity. Sell this underperforming asset and reallocate capital. Target this market for next acquisition based on portfolio gaps. Delay new purchases until leverage ratios stabilize.

Jason had never seen anything like it. Instead of guessing his next move, he was being shown a structured scaling path.

At first, he hesitated. He was used to making decisions based on instinct. But instinct had also led to stress, inconsistency, and slow growth. This system was different—it was analytical, structured, and objective.

He followed the recommendation.

He refinanced one property and unlocked significant equity. He sold another that had been draining his portfolio performance. Then he reinvested into a new market the AI identified as high-growth with strong cash flow potential.

The results were immediate.

Cash flow increased. Risk decreased. And for the first time, his portfolio felt balanced instead of chaotic.

Over the next few months, Jason stopped thinking in terms of individual deals. He started thinking in systems. Every decision was based on portfolio impact, not emotional preference. AI continuously guided him on when to acquire, when to hold, and when to reposition assets.

As his portfolio grew beyond fifteen properties, something unexpected happened. His workload decreased. Instead of managing more complexity, he was managing less. AI handled rent tracking, tenant communication, maintenance coordination, and financial reporting. His role shifted from operator to strategist.

One afternoon, Jason looked at his dashboard and noticed something that stopped him.

His portfolio was growing without increasing his workload.

New opportunities were being identified automatically. Capital was being optimized continuously. Risk was being managed in real time.

It didn't feel like he was building a portfolio anymore.

It felt like he was overseeing a system that built itself.

And for the first time, Jason understood the true meaning of scaling.

It wasn't about owning more properties.

It was about building something that could expand without breaking.

Chapter 7

AI Ecosystem Integration, Automation Mastery, and the Fully Self-Sustaining Rental Business

At the highest level of rental property investing, success is no longer defined by the number of properties owned or even the amount of monthly cash flow generated. Instead, true mastery is achieved when the entire investment system becomes self-sustaining, self-optimizing, and largely independent of daily human intervention. This is the stage where real estate investing transforms from an active business into an integrated ecosystem powered by artificial intelligence, automation, and strategic design. In this final stage of the rental investing framework, AI is no longer just a tool–it becomes the central nervous system of the entire portfolio.

An AI-integrated rental ecosystem connects every aspect of the investing process into a unified structure. Acquisition, financing, tenant screening, property management, rent optimization, maintenance coordination, portfolio analysis, and scaling strategies are no longer separate functions. Instead, they operate as interconnected components within a single intelligent system. This integration allows data to flow seamlessly between processes, enabling real-time decision-making and continuous optimization across the entire portfolio.

At the foundation of this ecosystem is automation. Automation is what allows investors to move beyond manual effort and into system-driven wealth creation. Tasks that once required constant attention—such as rent collection, maintenance scheduling, tenant communication, and financial reporting—are now handled automatically through AI-driven workflows. These systems operate continuously in the background, ensuring that properties remain functional, profitable, and efficient without requiring constant oversight.

One of the most powerful elements of AI ecosystem integration is real-time decision intelligence. Instead of reviewing monthly reports or reacting to problems after they occur, investors now receive live insights into portfolio performance. AI systems monitor cash flow fluctuations, tenant behavior patterns, maintenance trends, and market conditions simultaneously. When anomalies or opportunities arise, the system can either alert the investor or automatically execute predefined actions. This creates a level of responsiveness that traditional property management systems cannot match. Another critical aspect of ecosystem integration is financial synchronization. All income streams, expenses, debt obligations, and equity positions are tracked and analyzed in real time. AI consolidates this data into a unified financial dashboard that provides a complete view of portfolio health. This allows investors to understand not only how each property is performing individually, but how the entire system is performing as a whole. It also enables predictive financial modeling that shows how changes in interest rates, rent growth, or occupancy rates will impact long-term wealth.

AI also enhances strategic decision-making through continuous optimization. Instead of making isolated decisions, investors operate within a feedback loop where every action is analyzed for performance impact. If a property underperforms, AI can recommend adjustments such as rent changes, refinancing, or repositioning. If market conditions shift, the system can suggest new acquisition strategies or portfolio rebalancing actions. This creates a dynamic system that evolves over time rather than remaining static.

A fully integrated AI rental ecosystem also enables true scalability. In traditional investing, growth is limited by time, effort, and operational capacity. But when systems are automated and interconnected, scaling becomes a matter of strategy rather than workload. Investors can manage dozens or even hundreds of properties with minimal incremental effort because the system handles execution. The investor's role shifts from operator to architect—designing strategies rather than executing tasks.

Risk management is also elevated at this level. AI continuously monitors external economic indicators, property-level performance data, and tenant behavior patterns to detect potential risks before they escalate. This includes early warnings for market downturns, cash flow compression, tenant instability, or property-specific issues. By identifying risks early, the system allows for proactive adjustments that protect portfolio stability and long-term returns.

Perhaps the most transformative aspect of AI ecosystem integration is its ability to create true financial independence. When systems are fully automated and optimized, the investor is no longer tied to daily operations. Income becomes decoupled from time, and wealth generation becomes a function of system design rather than labor. This is the point where rental investing evolves into a fully passive, scalable wealth engine.

Ultimately, the AI-integrated rental ecosystem represents the highest level of modern real estate investing. It combines intelligence, automation, and strategic design into a single unified structure capable of operating continuously and efficiently. Investors who reach this stage are no longer managing properties—they are managing systems that manage properties for them.

This chapter marks the final evolution of AI-powered rental investing. In the closing story, we will see how an investor fully transitions from active management into complete system ownership, where the business operates independently and generates wealth without direct involvement.

"The Day the Business No Longer Needed Him"

When Adrian started investing in rental properties, he believed freedom would come from ownership. If he owned enough properties, he thought, he would eventually be free from financial stress and daily work. At first, that belief motivated him. He acquired his first property, then a second, then several more. Each one brought income, but also responsibility. And slowly, what he thought would create freedom began to feel like another job.

By the time Adrian reached ten properties, his life was consumed by management tasks. He was constantly responding to tenant messages, coordinating repairs, reviewing financial reports, and analyzing new deals. Even though his income had increased, so had his workload. He realized that he had not built a passive system—he had built a complex operating business that required constant attention.

One evening, exhausted from handling multiple maintenance issues, Adrian began searching for ways to simplify his operations. That search led him to AI ecosystem integration systems designed for real estate investors. Unlike anything he had seen before, these systems didn't just automate one part of the business—they connected everything.

Curious but cautious, Adrian decided to test it.

He connected his entire portfolio.

At first, nothing seemed different. But within minutes, he began to see something extraordinary. His properties were no longer isolated units. They were displayed as part of a single interconnected system. Cash flow, tenant activity, maintenance requests, loan balances, and performance metrics were all integrated into one live dashboard.

Then the system began to act.

A maintenance issue was automatically assigned to a vendor without his input. A late rent payment triggered an automated sequence of reminders and resolution steps. A property with declining performance was flagged with recommendations for rent adjustment. Another property showed refinancing opportunities based on current market rates.

Adrian didn't have to do anything.

The system was running itself.

At first, he felt uneasy. He was used to being in control. But as days passed, something unexpected happened. His stress decreased. His workload disappeared. And instead of reacting to problems, he was reviewing outcomes.

Weeks turned into months.

Adrian stopped managing tasks and started reviewing system performance. The AI handled tenant communication, maintenance coordination, financial tracking, and even deal sourcing for future acquisitions. His portfolio continued to grow, but his involvement continued to shrink.

One morning, he opened his dashboard and noticed something that made him pause.

No urgent tasks. No tenant issues. No pending decisions.

Everything was operating normally. He leaned back and realized something he had never experienced before.

His business was running without him.

Not struggling. Not needing supervision. Simply operating.

That was the moment everything changed.

Adrian was no longer a landlord.

He was no longer an operator.

He was no longer even managing a portfolio.

He was overseeing a system that managed itself.

And for the first time, he understood what true freedom actually meant.

It wasn't owning properties.

It wasn't collecting rent.

It wasn't even scaling a portfolio.

It was building something that no longer needed you to survive.

And Adrian had finally built it.

Chapter 8

AI Financing Strategies, DSCR Leverage, and Capital Optimization for Scalable Rental Growth

At this stage of AI-driven rental investing, the focus shifts from managing properties and systems to mastering the flow of capital that fuels expansion. Financing is the engine behind every acquisition, and without a strategic approach to leverage, even the best-performing portfolio will eventually plateau. Traditional financing methods often limit investors based on personal income, debt-to-income ratios, and rigid underwriting criteria. Artificial intelligence fundamentally changes this by optimizing financing strategies, identifying the best lending structures, and aligning capital usage with portfolio performance in real time.

One of the most important advancements in modern real estate financing is DSCR lending, where loan qualification is based on the income generated by the property rather than the borrower's personal financial profile. This shift allows investors to scale far beyond traditional limitations. However, selecting the right DSCR structure, lender, and terms requires precision. AI systems analyze rental income projections, debt coverage ratios, interest rate environments, and lender-specific guidelines to match each property with the most efficient financing option available.

In a traditional environment, investors often rely on brokers or manual comparisons to evaluate loan options, which can lead to suboptimal financing decisions. AI eliminates this inefficiency by instantly comparing multiple lending scenarios across different institutions. It evaluates not only interest rates but also closing costs, prepayment penalties, loan-to-value ratios, and long-term cash flow impact. This allows investors to choose financing structures that maximize both monthly income and long-term equity growth.

Another critical aspect of AI-driven financing is leverage optimization. Leverage can accelerate wealth creation when used correctly, but it can also increase risk if mismanaged. AI systems simulate different leverage scenarios across an entire portfolio, showing how debt levels impact cash flow stability, risk exposure, and scalability potential. This allows investors to maintain an optimal balance between growth and financial security rather than overextending during expansion phases. Capital efficiency is another key focus in AI financing strategies. Every dollar tied up in underperforming assets represents lost opportunity. AI identifies capital inefficiencies within a portfolio and recommends strategies to redeploy funds more effectively. This may include refinancing properties to extract equity, consolidating debt for better terms, or selling assets that no longer align with portfolio goals. The result is a continuous cycle of capital recycling that fuels ongoing expansion.

AI also enhances pre-qualification and underwriting efficiency. Instead of manually preparing loan applications or guessing approval likelihood, investors can use AI systems to simulate lender responses before submitting applications. This reduces rejection risk and ensures that applications are tailored to meet specific lender criteria. It also accelerates closing timelines, allowing investors to act quickly on high-quality opportunities.

Interest rate strategy is another area where AI plays a critical role. Even small differences in interest rates can have significant long-term effects on cash flow and wealth accumulation. AI monitors rate trends, market forecasts, and lender behavior patterns to recommend optimal timing for refinancing or new acquisitions. This ensures that investors lock in favorable rates and avoid unnecessary financing costs during volatile market periods. Portfolio-level financing optimization is where AI truly demonstrates its power. Instead of evaluating loans individually, AI analyzes how each financing decision impacts the entire portfolio. This includes aggregate debt exposure, combined cash flow performance, and overall risk distribution. By viewing financing holistically, investors can make decisions that strengthen the entire system rather than optimizing isolated deals.

Another major advantage of AI in financing is speed. Real estate opportunities often require fast decision-making. AI dramatically reduces the time required to evaluate loan options, structure deals, and assess feasibility. This allows investors to move quickly in competitive markets while maintaining financial discipline and accuracy.

Ultimately, AI-powered financing transforms leverage from a reactive tool into a strategic advantage. Investors are no longer limited by traditional underwriting constraints or slow manual processes. Instead, they operate within a dynamic financing ecosystem that continuously identifies the best capital structures for growth, stability, and scalability.

In the next and final chapter, we will bring everything together into a fully unified system—showing how AI integrates acquisitions, financing, management, and scaling into a complete automated real estate empire that operates continuously and independently.

"The Deal That Changed Everything"

When Carlos started his real estate journey, financing was always the most frustrating part of the process. He could find decent properties, analyze deals, and even manage tenants fairly well. But every time he tried to scale, he hit the same wall: lenders. His personal income limited how many properties he could finance, and every new loan felt like a long, stressful negotiation filled with paperwork, delays, and uncertainty.

At first, Carlos accepted this as normal. He assumed that real estate investing simply required patience and persistence with banks. But as he tried to grow from three properties to six, and then to ten, the limitations became impossible to ignore. Even profitable deals were slipping away because financing took too long or didn't qualify under traditional guidelines.

One day, while researching ways to improve his funding strategy, Carlos discovered AI-driven financing optimization tools. Unlike anything he had used before, these systems didn't just show loan rates—they analyzed entire financing ecosystems in real time. DSCR options, non-QM lenders, interest rate projections, leverage impact, and portfolio-level debt analysis were all integrated into one system. Skeptical but desperate for a solution, Carlos tested it on his next potential deal. He entered the property details and waited.

Within seconds, the system produced a full financing breakdown. It showed multiple loan structures from different lenders, ranked by profitability, cash flow impact, and long-term cost efficiency. One option stood out immediately—a DSCR loan structure that offered better leverage, lower long-term interest cost, and improved monthly cash flow compared to anything he had previously used.

But the system didn't stop there.

It also showed him something he hadn't considered. If he adjusted his financing strategy across two existing properties, he could unlock enough equity to acquire the new property without increasing his personal financial exposure.

Carlos had never thought that way before.

He had always looked at deals one at a time. But now he was seeing his entire portfolio as a connected financial system.

He followed the recommendation.

He refinanced one property, adjusted the structure on another, and secured the DSCR loan on the new acquisition exactly as the AI suggested. The results were immediate.

Cash flow improved across the portfolio. His leverage became more efficient. And most importantly, he was no longer constrained by his personal income.

Over the next few months, Carlos began using AI for every financing decision. Before submitting any loan application, he would run scenarios through the system. It told him which lenders were most likely to approve him, which structures would maximize cash flow, and when to refinance for optimal equity extraction.

For the first time, financing stopped being a barrier.

It became a strategy.

As his portfolio grew, Carlos realized something powerful. He was no longer thinking like a borrower. He was thinking like a capital strategist. Every property was part of a larger financial structure. Every loan was a tool for expansion. And every decision was guided by data instead of limitation.

One evening, Carlos reviewed his updated portfolio. He noticed something that made him pause. He had acquired three new properties in the last year—without increasing his personal income requirements, without stress, and without financial strain. It wasn't because he earned more. It was because his system financed smarter.

He leaned back and realized the truth.

He had not been limited by money.

He had been limited by strategy.

And once AI removed that limitation, everything changed.

Carlos was no longer trying to qualify for deals.

He was structuring them.

And for the first time, capital was no longer something he chased—it was something he controlled.

Chapter 9

AI Portfolio Management, Risk Control, and Automated Wealth Scaling Systems

At the highest level of AI-powered rental investing, success is no longer defined by acquisition, financing, or even individual property performance. Instead, it is defined by the ability to manage an entire portfolio as a living financial system that continuously adapts, self-corrects, and scales over time. This is where artificial intelligence becomes essential not as a supporting tool, but as the central control system for long-term wealth creation. In this stage, investors shift from managing properties to managing intelligence-driven ecosystems that operate across multiple markets, asset classes, and financial structures simultaneously.

Portfolio management in traditional real estate investing is often fragmented and reactive. Investors review spreadsheets, monthly reports, and property-level updates to understand performance. Decisions are made after problems occur, not before. This creates inefficiencies, missed opportunities, and unnecessary risk exposure. AI transforms portfolio management into a real-time, predictive system where performance is continuously monitored, analyzed, and optimized without manual intervention.

One of the most powerful components of AI portfolio management is real-time performance tracking. Instead of waiting for end-of-month reports, investors now have access to live dashboards that show cash flow, occupancy rates, maintenance costs, equity growth, and debt exposure across the entire portfolio. This allows for immediate awareness of any changes in performance, enabling faster and more accurate decision-making.

Beyond tracking, AI introduces predictive risk modeling. Rather than reacting to issues after they occur, investors can anticipate potential problems before they materialize. AI systems analyze historical trends, tenant behavior patterns, market conditions, and economic indicators to forecast risks such as rising vacancy rates, declining rent values, or increased maintenance costs. This predictive capability allows investors to take proactive steps to protect their portfolio.

Another critical aspect of AI-driven portfolio management is automated optimization. In traditional investing, portfolios often become stagnant over time, with no structured process for improving performance. AI changes this by continuously evaluating each asset and recommending adjustments. These adjustments may include refinancing underperforming properties, increasing rent in high-demand areas, selling assets that no longer align with strategy, or reinvesting capital into higher-performing markets.

AI also enhances diversification strategy. A well-structured portfolio is not only profitable but also balanced across geography, property type, and risk level. AI evaluates portfolio concentration and identifies overexposure in specific markets or asset classes. It then recommends diversification strategies that reduce risk while maintaining or increasing returns. This ensures that investors are not overly dependent on a single market or economic condition.

Another major advancement is automated decision execution. In advanced systems, AI does not simply recommend actions—it can execute them within predefined parameters. For example, it can adjust rent pricing based on market shifts, initiate refinancing processes when equity thresholds are met, or trigger maintenance workflows when predictive models indicate potential system failure. This level of automation significantly reduces the need for manual oversight.

AI also plays a key role in long-term wealth forecasting. Instead of focusing only on current cash flow, investors can project portfolio performance years into the future. These projections include equity growth, loan amortization, rent appreciation, and market expansion scenarios. This long-term visibility allows investors to make decisions based on generational wealth creation rather than short-term gains.

Risk control is another foundational pillar of AI portfolio management. Every portfolio carries exposure to economic cycles, interest rate fluctuations, tenant instability, and property-specific risks. AI continuously evaluates these factors and assigns risk scores to each asset and to the portfolio as a whole. When risk levels increase, the system provides immediate recommendations to rebalance or mitigate exposure.

Perhaps the most transformative aspect of AI portfolio management is scalability without complexity. In traditional investing, adding more properties increases workload linearly or even exponentially. In AI-driven systems, scaling does not significantly increase operational complexity because automation absorbs the additional workload. This allows investors to grow from a few properties to large portfolios without becoming overwhelmed. Ultimately, AI portfolio management represents the transition from active investing to system-based wealth engineering. Investors are no longer managing properties individually—they are managing intelligent systems that manage properties for them. This is the stage where real estate becomes truly scalable, predictable, and sustainable as a long-term wealth vehicle.

In the final chapter, we will bring together everything from the entire series and explore how AI transforms real estate investing into a fully automated wealth engine capable of generating income, scaling assets, and operating independently in a continuously evolving financial ecosystem.

"The Portfolio That Learned to Think"

When Nathan first entered real estate investing, he thought success would come from buying the right properties. He spent years studying neighborhoods, analyzing deals, speaking with lenders, and building what he believed was a strong portfolio. And for a while, it worked. His income grew slowly, his properties appreciated, and he felt like he was on the right path.

But as his portfolio expanded, something changed.

What once felt manageable began to feel overwhelming. Reports piled up. Expenses became harder to track. Some properties performed well while others lagged behind. He couldn't clearly understand why certain decisions worked and others didn't. Despite owning more assets, he didn't feel more in control—he felt more reactive.

Every month became a cycle of reviewing numbers, fixing problems, and trying to stay ahead of issues that always seemed to appear unexpectedly.

Nathan realized he wasn't building a system.

He was managing chaos.

One evening, after spending hours trying to analyze his portfolio performance, Nathan discovered an AI portfolio management platform designed for real estate investors. At first, he was skeptical. He had used software before, but nothing had ever truly simplified his workload.

Still, he decided to try.

He connected all of his properties to the system.

Within minutes, everything changed.

For the first time, Nathan saw his entire portfolio displayed as a single unified system. Cash flow, equity, debt exposure, tenant performance, maintenance trends, and market positioning were all visible in one place. But what surprised him most was not the data—it was the insights.

The system didn't just show him what was happening.

It told him what was going to happen.

One property was flagged for future cash flow decline due to rising maintenance costs in the area. Another showed strong refinancing potential that could unlock significant equity. A third was underperforming relative to similar assets and needed rent optimization.

Nathan had never seen his portfolio like this before.

He had always looked backward.

Now he was looking forward.

The system began recommending actions. Refinance this property. Adjust rent here. Consider selling this asset. Reinvest capital into a stronger market. At first, Nathan hesitated. These were not small adjustments—they were strategic shifts.

But the logic was undeniable.

He followed the recommendations. Over the next several months, something remarkable happened. His portfolio stopped feeling fragmented. Instead of reacting to problems, he began receiving guidance before problems even occurred. Cash flow stabilized. Risk decreased. Efficiency improved.

But the most surprising change was not financial.

It was mental.

Nathan no longer felt overwhelmed.

He no longer spent nights reviewing spreadsheets or chasing issues.

Instead, he reviewed system insights.

The portfolio was managing itself.

One afternoon, Nathan opened his dashboard and noticed something that made him pause. There were no urgent alerts. No missed issues. No critical problems to solve.

Everything was operating normally.

He scrolled through the data again, expecting to find something he had missed.

There was nothing.

For the first time in years, he realized he didn't have to do anything.

The system was doing it all.

Not because he stopped working.

But because the system had learned how to think.

Nathan leaned back and understood something deeply.

He was no longer managing properties.

He was overseeing an intelligent financial system that managed itself.

And in that moment, everything about real estate investing changed forever.

Chapter 10

The Fully Automated AI Real Estate Empire — Building a Self-Sustaining Wealth System That Runs 24/7

At the highest level of modern real estate investing, the goal is no longer simply to acquire properties, optimize cash flow, or even scale a portfolio. The true endgame is the creation of a fully automated AI-driven real estate empire—an interconnected system where acquisition, financing, property management, tenant operations, portfolio optimization, and capital recycling all function together without requiring constant human intervention. This is where investing evolves into engineering, and where wealth creation becomes a byproduct of systems rather than effort.

A fully automated real estate empire is built on one foundational principle: integration. Every component of the business must communicate with every other component in real time. Acquisition systems feed data into financing models. Financing systems inform portfolio allocation. Property management systems report performance back into optimization engines. AI acts as the central nervous system, continuously analyzing inputs, making decisions, and improving outcomes across the entire ecosystem.

In traditional investing, these functions operate in isolation. A property is purchased, then managed separately, then refinanced or sold independently. This creates inefficiency and fragmentation. AI eliminates this separation by unifying all functions into a single intelligent structure. The result is a system that behaves like a living organism—constantly adapting, learning, and improving.

One of the most important components of a fully automated empire is autonomous deal flow. Instead of manually searching for properties, AI continuously scans markets, identifies opportunities, evaluates cash flow potential, and filters deals based on investor-defined criteria. These opportunities are then ranked and presented only when they meet strict portfolio requirements. This transforms deal sourcing from an active process into a passive, always-on pipeline.

Financing automation is another critical pillar. In a traditional model, investors manually evaluate loan options, compare lenders, and negotiate terms. In an AI-driven system, financing decisions are optimized automatically based on portfolio structure, interest rate conditions, DSCR ratios, and equity positions. The system determines when to refinance, when to leverage, and when to hold capital for future expansion. This ensures that every dollar of capital is used at its highest efficiency.

Property management becomes fully autonomous at this level. Tenant screening, lease approvals, rent collection, maintenance coordination, and communication are all handled through integrated AI workflows. Tenants interact with automated systems that resolve issues instantly, schedule repairs, and process payments without delays. This removes the operational burden from the investor entirely and ensures consistent tenant satisfaction across the portfolio.

Portfolio optimization is continuously running in the background. AI evaluates each asset not just individually, but as part of a larger system. It identifies underperforming properties, recommends strategic adjustments, and rebalances portfolio exposure across markets and asset types. If one market begins to weaken, the system adjusts acquisition priorities. If another market strengthens, it reallocates capital toward that opportunity automatically.

Risk management becomes predictive rather than reactive. AI continuously monitors economic indicators, interest rate trends, rental demand shifts, and property-level performance. It identifies risks before they impact cash flow and executes protective strategies such as refinancing, rent adjustments, or asset repositioning. This creates a portfolio that is not only profitable but resilient across market cycles.

Scaling within a fully automated system becomes exponential rather than linear. Because operations are automated, adding new properties does not significantly increase workload. The system absorbs new assets, integrates them into the portfolio, and optimizes them automatically. This allows investors to grow from a handful of properties to large-scale portfolios without operational bottlenecks.

Perhaps the most powerful outcome of AI integration is financial independence decoupled from time. Income is no longer tied to effort. The system generates revenue continuously, even when the investor is not actively involved. Decisions are made based on data, not emotion. Execution is handled by automation, not manual labor.

At this level, the investor's role fundamentally changes. They are no longer a manager or operator. They become a system architect—designing rules, setting parameters, and refining strategy while the AI handles execution. Wealth creation becomes a matter of system design rather than daily work.

Ultimately, the fully automated AI real estate empire represents the final evolution of rental investing. It is a self-sustaining financial ecosystem capable of acquiring assets, optimizing performance, managing operations, and scaling wealth continuously. It does not sleep, it does not slow down, and it does not rely on constant human input.

This is the future of real estate investing: not ownership of properties, but ownership of systems that build, manage, and expand wealth automatically.

"The Day the Empire Outgrew the Investor"

When Ethan started investing in real estate, he had a simple goal. He wanted freedom. Freedom from financial stress, freedom from working long hours, and freedom to spend more time with his family. Like many investors, he believed that owning enough properties would eventually give him that freedom.

At first, everything felt exciting. He bought his first rental property, then a second, then several more. Each deal felt like progress. Each closing felt like success. But as his portfolio grew, something unexpected happened. The more properties he owned, the less free he felt.

He was constantly managing something. A tenant issue here. A maintenance request there. A financing decision in between. Even when properties were performing well, his attention never stopped being required. Instead of building freedom, he had built responsibility.

One night, after reviewing yet another set of property reports, Ethan realized something uncomfortable.

He wasn't free.

He was busy.

That was the moment he started searching for something different. Not another property strategy, not another financing trick, but a way to remove himself from the constant cycle of management. That search led him to an AI real estate automation system designed to integrate every part of a rental portfolio into one intelligent ecosystem.

At first, he didn't believe it was possible. A system that could manage acquisitions, financing, tenants, maintenance, and portfolio performance all at once sounded unrealistic. But curiosity pushed him forward. He connected his entire portfolio.

And within minutes, everything changed.

For the first time, Ethan wasn't looking at individual properties. He was looking at a living system. Every property was connected. Every financial flow was tracked. Every tenant interaction was monitored. Every risk was calculated in real time.

Then the system began to act.

A maintenance issue was automatically assigned and resolved without his input. Rent payments were processed and tracked automatically. A refinancing opportunity was flagged and executed based on predefined parameters. A weak-performing property was identified and repositioned for better performance.

Ethan didn't touch anything.

The system handled everything.

Days passed.

Then weeks.

And something strange happened.

Nothing broke. In fact, everything improved.

Cash flow became more stable. Tenant satisfaction increased. Maintenance costs decreased. Portfolio performance became more consistent than anything Ethan had ever managed manually.

But the most surprising change was not in the numbers.

It was in his life.

For the first time in years, Ethan wasn't reacting to problems. He wasn't managing chaos. He wasn't spending his days fixing issues or making urgent decisions.

He was observing.

One morning, he opened his dashboard expecting to find something that needed his attention.

There was nothing.

No alerts.

No problems.

No decisions waiting.

Just a system operating exactly as designed.

He sat there for a long moment, staring at the screen.

And then it hit him.

He was no longer running a real estate business.

The business was running itself.

Not because he stepped away.

But because he had built something that no longer needed him to function.

The empire had outgrown the investor.

And instead of collapsing without him...

It thrived.

Final Comments

The Future of AI Real Estate Investing and What Comes Next

As this series comes to a close, it is important to step back and recognize what has actually been built through these chapters. This is not simply a guide to rental property investing, nor is it just an introduction to artificial intelligence in real estate. What you have explored is a complete shift in how wealth is created, managed, and scaled in the modern world. The traditional boundaries of real estate investing—time, location, experience, and capital limitations—have been fundamentally redefined by AI-driven systems. The result is a new model of investing where intelligence, automation, and structured decision-making replace guesswork and manual effort.

For decades, real estate investing has been viewed as a hands-on business. Success was believed to come from experience, hustle, and the ability to manage complexity through personal effort. Investors were taught to analyze deals manually, manage tenants directly, and rely heavily on intuition. While this approach worked for many, it also created ceilings. Growth was slow, mistakes were costly, and scaling often required overwhelming levels of effort. What AI introduces is not just efficiency, but a complete restructuring of how the entire system operates.

Across all ten books in this series, a clear progression has emerged. First, AI helps identify opportunities faster. Then it helps analyze and evaluate those opportunities with precision. Next, it improves decision-making in financing, tenant selection, and property management. Eventually, it evolves into full portfolio management, automation, and ecosystem integration. At the highest level, it becomes a fully autonomous system capable of operating independently while continuously optimizing itself. This progression is not theoretical—it is already happening in real markets today.

One of the most important lessons from this series is that real estate success is no longer about working harder, but about building better systems. Investors who continue to rely solely on manual processes will find themselves increasingly limited in speed, scale, and performance. Meanwhile, those who adopt AI-driven systems will operate with greater efficiency, lower risk, and significantly higher scalability. The gap between system-based investors and traditional investors will continue to widen over time.

Another key takeaway is that data has replaced intuition as the foundation of decision-making. In the past, investors often relied on experience and gut feeling to guide their choices. While experience still has value, it is no longer enough on its own. AI systems can process thousands of variables simultaneously, uncover hidden patterns, and generate insights that are impossible to replicate manually. This does not remove human judgment—it enhances it by providing clarity and structure where uncertainty once existed.

It is also important to understand that automation does not eliminate control; it enhances it. Many investors initially fear that automation means losing control over their investments. In reality, the opposite is true. Automation removes repetitive tasks, reduces emotional decision-making, and allows investors to focus on higher-level strategy. Instead of being trapped in daily operations, investors gain the ability to design, refine, and scale systems that operate independently.

As AI continues to evolve, the future of real estate investing will become increasingly system-driven. Properties will not be managed individually but as parts of interconnected financial ecosystems. Financing will be optimized dynamically based on portfolio performance. Tenant management will become fully automated. Market selection will be guided by predictive intelligence rather than historical data alone. Investors will operate less like operators and more like system architects.

This shift also changes what success looks like. Success will no longer be defined solely by the number of properties owned or the amount of income generated. Instead, it will be defined by the efficiency, scalability, and autonomy of the systems built. A small, highly optimized AI-driven portfolio may outperform a large, manually managed portfolio simply because of structure and intelligence.

However, it is important to recognize that AI is not a replacement for decision-making—it is an amplifier. The quality of outcomes still depends on the quality of inputs, strategy, and design. Investors who understand how to properly structure their systems will gain a significant advantage. Those who misuse or underutilize AI will not see the same level of benefit. The technology is powerful, but it still requires direction.

Looking forward, the opportunity in real estate is not diminishing—it is expanding. AI is lowering barriers to entry, increasing efficiency, and opening access to strategies that were once reserved for institutional investors. Individuals now have the ability to build scalable, automated portfolios that operate at levels previously unreachable without large teams or capital resources. The most important shift, however, is mental. Investors must begin to see real estate not as isolated transactions, but as interconnected systems. Every property is part of a larger ecosystem. Every financing decision affects portfolio performance. Every operational process contributes to or detracts from overall scalability. Once this systems-based thinking is adopted, the entire approach to investing changes permanently.

As you move forward beyond this series, the key is not to simply apply what you have learned, but to continue evolving it. AI tools will improve. Markets will shift. Strategies will adapt. But the core principle will remain the same: wealth is built through systems that work without constant intervention.

The future belongs to investors who think in systems, act with data, and build with automation. Those who embrace this shift will not just participate in real estate investing—they will redefine it.

And as this series concludes, one truth remains clear. The goal was never just to teach you how to invest in real estate. The goal was to show you how to build something that continues to grow, adapt, and generate wealth long after individual effort is removed from the equation.

www.ingramcontent.com/pod-product-compliance
Ingram Content Group UK Ltd.
Pitfield, Milton Keynes, MK11 3LW, UK
UKHW010012031026
15589UKWH00008B/1623

9 798295 885266